SECRETS OF WORLD WAR II

BY SEAN McCOLLUM

CAPSTONE PRESS
a capstone imprint

Edge Books are published by Capstone Press,
1710 Roe Crest Drive, North Mankato, Minnesota 56003
www.mycapstone.com

Library of Congress Cataloging-in-Publication Data
Cataloging-in-Publication data is on file
at the Library of Congress website.

Editorial Credits
Nate LeBoutillier, editor; Steve Mead, designer;
Pam Mistakos, media researcher, Laura Manthe, production specialist

Photo Credits
Bridgeman Images: Inflatable Light Tank used in England for Operation Fortitude,
1944 (Operation Overlord), 13, The Stapleton Collection, 23 bottom; Getty Images: The
Stanley Weston Archive, 16, Universal History Archive, 23 top right; Granger: ullstein
bild/Granger, NYC - All rights reserved, 17; Newscom: Everett Collection, 15, R Chandler
News Syndication, 25; Shutterstock: Dmitrijs Mihejevs, 18, Everett Collection, cover,
Everett Historical, 2-3, 4-5, 7, 9, 10-11, 14, 19, 26, 27, 28; Wikimedia: Executive Office of
the President of the United States, 20, U.S. Navy, 21, Naval Historical Center, 24

Shuttertsock: Design Elements, Davor Ratkovic, javarman, STILLFX, yoshi0511

Printed and bound in China.
007891

TABLE OF CONTENTS

THE ROAD TO TOTAL WAR

Germany was in ruins after its defeat in World War I (1914–1918). This helped give rise to the Nazi Party. The Nazis promised to make their country powerful again. In the 1930s, they seized control of the government with Adolf Hitler as their leader.

Germany secretly began rebuilding its military forces. Afraid of getting into another disastrous war, other countries were slow to confront the threat.

On the other side of the world, Imperial Japan was pursuing goals similar to Nazi Germany's. In the 1930s, Japanese troops invaded parts of China. In 1939, Germany launched its plan to conquer Europe. Country after country was drawn into the fighting.

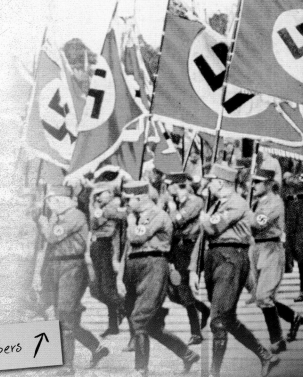

Nazi Party members →

World War II was fought on a huge scale. It featured sneak attacks, secret codes, and top-secret spy missions. It unleashed the deadliest secret weapon ever made. Military forces were not the only targets. It soon became clear that cities and **civilians** would not be spared.

It was total war.

civilian—a person who is not in the military

SNEAK ATTACKS— FAST AND FURIOUS

World War II started with a series of surprise attacks. Both Nazi Germany and Imperial Japan hoped to surprise their enemies in order to get the upper hand.

"BLITZKRIEG"

On September 1, 1939, German forces invaded Poland, starting World War II. The German offensive teamed infantry with fast-moving armor. Stuka dive bombers struck from the sky. These attacks pierced the Poles' defenses then circled back and destroyed them. British reporters called the strategy *blitzkrieg*, German for "lightning war." Germany crushed Polish resistance in less than a month. The rest of Europe watched with alarm. The German war machine seemed unstoppable.

OPERATION BARBAROSSA

In June 1941, Nazi Germany launched Operation Barbarossa against the Soviet Union. It was a shocking betrayal. The Nazis and Soviets had signed a deal in 1939 that they would not attack each other. In fact, the Soviet army joined the Germans to overrun Poland. By early 1941, though, the Germans controlled most of Western Europe. This freed German forces to turn on the Soviet Union with the largest invasion force in history.

ALLIED POWERS (MAIN COUNTRIES)	AXIS POWERS (MAIN COUNTRIES)
Great Britain (and its colonies) Soviet Union United States France China	Germany Japan Italy

FIGHTING FACT Stuka planes had wailing sirens. The sound effect made their force even more terrifying.

↑ German Army engineers cross the Vistula River in Poland.

JAPAN ATTACKS PEARL HARBOR

Japan's **ultimate** goal was to control all of Southeast Asia. In 1941 it secretly set in motion a bold plan to drive British and U.S. forces from its side of the Pacific Ocean.

On November 26, 1941, the main Japanese attack fleet secretly sailed from Japan. Its target was the U.S. naval base at Pearl Harbor, Hawaii. The fleet featured six aircraft carriers. Before dawn on December 7, they were in range. More than 350 planes took off from the Japanese carriers. The Americans were taken by complete surprise when these aircraft swept down from the sky. Dropping torpedoes and bombs, they destroyed 188 U.S. planes and sunk or damaged nearly 20 ships. The attack triggered U.S. entry into the war.

SOUTHEAST ASIA FALLS

Japanese forces staged surprise attacks across Southeast Asia within days of striking Pearl Harbor. They invaded Hong Kong, a British colony. They seized U.S. bases on Guam and Wake Island. Within three months they had captured the British stronghold of Singapore and the U.S.-controlled Philippines. By early 1942, Japan had much of the region in its grip.

FIGHTING FACT Japan used five top-secret mini-subs as part of its attack on Pearl Harbor. Each carried two torpedoes. Some evidence suggests one succeeded in torpedoing a U.S. battleship.

The battered U.S.S. California moves into Pearl Harbor.

ultimate—greatest, most important

OPERATION URANUS

Soviet forces fell back as the German army pushed eastward in 1941–42. However, the Soviets were able to spring a trap at the **besieged** city of Stalingrad. Called Operation Uranus, it stunned German commanders in November 1942. Soviet units pretended to be building defenses, but instead attacked from the north. The next day a second group of Soviet forces sprang forward from the south. Soon the Soviets had encircled more than 250,000 enemy soldiers. The Soviet victory finally handed the Nazi war machine a major defeat.

German infantry moves into a burning Soviet village. ↓

THE BATTLE OF MIDWAY

In June, 1942, Japanese and U.S. fleets steamed toward a major battle near Midway Island. The Japanese force included four aircraft carriers, the Americans three. The ships sent wave after wave of torpedo bombers at the enemy. At one point U.S. bombers hit the Japanese carriers while their decks were jammed with refueling planes. This caused mass destruction. In the end, four Japanese carriers sank while the U.S. lost one. The Japanese had hoped to lure the Americans into a trap and destroy its all-important aircraft carriers. The opposite happened. Now the US had the upper hand in the battle for the Pacific.

FIGHTING FACT

The U.S. had broken Japan's naval codes before the Battle of Midway. Therefore, U.S. forces went into the fight knowing of Japanese plans to capture Midway Island.

besiege—to surround with armed forces

CHAPTER TWO

SECRETS BEHIND THE FRONT LINES

One goal in warfare is to keep the enemy off-balance and confused. **Deception** played an important role throughout World War II.

THE DOOLITTLE RAID

After Pearl Harbor the U.S. was desperate for a chance to strike back. Japan, though, seemed out of reach. Then the U.S. Navy proposed a daring, top-secret raid. On April 18, 1942, 16 B-25 bombers roared off the deck of an aircraft carrier 650 miles (1,050 kilometers) from Japan. Led by Colonel Jimmy Doolittle the pilots flew for Tokyo, Japan's capital. The aircraft dropped their bombs then crash-landed in China. The bombing did little damage but it shocked the Japanese. It also gave a big boost to American spirits.

FIGHTING FACT

In 1944 and 1945, Japan released more than 9,000 "balloon bombs." Air currents carried these bomb-carrying hydrogen balloons from Japan over North America. Only one exploded, killing a group of six people who found a crashed balloon in the state of Oregon.

Soldiers display an inflatable tank used in Operation Fortitude.

OPERATION FORTITUDE

In 1944, the Allies executed Operation Fortitude in locations throughout Europe. This plan created a phantom army of fake equipment to trick the Germans. It included inflatable tanks and planes built of wood. The Allies sent fake radio messages to support the hoax. The goal was to fool Axis spies about Allied strength and where the Allies planned to strike in Europe. The trickery helped the Allies succeed in landing a huge invasion force at Normandy, France, in June 1944.

deception—something that makes people believe what is not true; a lie

ENIGMA AND ULTRA

German commanders used the Enigma machine to transmit their most important orders. It looked like a clunky keyboard, but Enigma scrambled messages in complex ways. Only another programmed Enigma machine could **decipher** them.

German leaders believed their codes were unbreakable. However, **cryptologists** from Poland, Britain, and France gradually cracked them. This top-secret program was code-named Ultra. Their efforts were aided when the British captured a German submarine in 1941. A working Enigma machine was found on board. As the war wore on, the Allies knew more and more about German plans.

Enigma machine →

NAVAJO CODE TALKERS

Early in the war the U.S. Marines recruited Navajo men. They created a code using their very complex Native American language. It had never been written down. Few non-Navajo had ever heard it. The Navajo Code Talkers allowed Marine units to transmit messages quickly. Standard secret messages had to be coded and decoded, taking precious time. Japanese codebreakers were baffled by words and sounds they had never heard. After an important battle, one U.S. officer said, "Were it not for the Navajos, the Marines would never have taken Iwo Jima."

↓ Navajo Code Talkers

decipher—to figure out something that is written in code or is hard to understand

cryptologist—someone who studies codes

OPERATION GUNNERSIDE

Secret missions had the potential to change the course of the war—and history. In February 1943 a small team of Norwegian **commandoes** sneaked into a heavily guarded factory in German-**occupied** Norway. They rigged explosives then escaped. They skied 250 miles (400 km) to safety while being hunted by German troops. The explosion destroyed the equipment German scientists were using to make a chemical known as "heavy water." This was an important ingredient for an atomic bomb. Operation *Gunnerside*, as it was called, helped block the Nazis from developing this super-weapon.

SPY CATCHER

Moe Berg played pro baseball for 15 years. He was a decent catcher but a below-average hitter. He was also called "the brainiest guy in baseball." He spoke several languages and knew everything about world history and current events. Once the war started; he went to work as a spy for the U.S. He served undercover to keep tabs on Germany's efforts to build an atomic bomb.

OPERATION VALKYRIE

By 1944 the tide of war had turned against Germany. A group of German officers feared Hitler was leading the country to disaster. They plotted to take control of the government and make peace with the Allies. The first step was to kill Hitler in an operation called Valkyrie. On July 20, 1944, Colonel Claus von Stauffenberg sneaked a time bomb into a meeting, then left. The bomb blew the room to pieces and killed four people. Hitler, though, had been shielded by a heavy table. He suffered minor burns and a wounded arm. Operation Valkyrie had failed.

↓ Adolph Hitler's headquarters lay in ruins after failed Operation Valkyrie.

commando—specially trained soldier used for secret missions

occupy—to take possession or control by military invasion

THE FINAL SOLUTION

After Hitler took power in 1933, a nightmare unfolded in Europe. The Nazis imprisoned and killed people they considered "undesirable." Jews were at the top of the list. The Nazis blamed them for all of Germany's troubles.

"The Final Solution" was the Nazis' secret plan to wipe out Europe's Jews. Special units rounded up Jewish men, women, and children. Some were executed on the spot. Some were forced to work in slave-labor camps. The Nazis also built extermination camps where prisoners were murdered with poison gas. This horrific episode in human history is remembered as the Holocaust.

Auschwitz extermination camp

Prisoners stand in line at a concentration camp in Buchenwald.

RESCUE OF THE DANISH JEWS

Nazi Germany invaded Denmark in April 1940. Three years later, the Nazis ordered all of the country's 7,800 Jews to be **deported** to concentration camps. The Danish resistance movement sprang into action. Danes helped hide their Jewish friends and neighbors. They were then smuggled in boats to Sweden, a **neutral** country. The rescue effort saved most of Denmark's Jews from certain death.

deport—to forcefully send someone out of the country

neutral—not supporting or agreeing with either side of a disagreement or competition

Holocaust—the killing of millions of Jews and other people by the Nazis during World War II

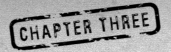

CHAPTER THREE

NEW WEAPONS FOR A NEW KIND OF WAR

World War II introduced tactics and classes of weapons that revolutionized warfare.

SINKING THE *BISMARCK*

Before World War II, battleships were the kings of sea power. But a new kind of ship, the aircraft carrier with its planes, forever changed naval warfare. In May 1941, a powerful, new German battleship called *Bismarck* steamed into the Atlantic Ocean. It soon destroyed the British battlecruiser HMS *Hood*. Before *Bismarck* could escape, torpedo bombers from a British aircraft carrier caught up with it. A single torpedo wrecked *Bismark's* rudder so it could not steer. British ships then closed in for the kill.

FIGHTING FACT

In 1944 the USS *Finback*, a *Gato*-class submarine, rescued downed torpedo-bomber pilot George H. W. Bush. Forty-four years later Bush was elected president of the United States.

← U.S.S. Finback

GATO-CLASS SUBMARINES

In 1941, the U.S. introduced *Gato*-class submarines. Seventy-seven were built, and most served in the Pacific. These subs were big, tough, and stealthy. They could escape the enemy by diving as deep as 300 feet (90 meters). Their crews of 60–80 sailors could stay on patrol for 75 days at a time. This new class of submarine hurt the Japanese navy by sinking many military and supply ships.

RADAR AND THE BATTLE OF BRITAIN

By mid-1940, only Great Britain still stood against Nazi Germany in Western Europe. The *Luftwaffe*, Germany's air force, sent wave after wave of bombers and fighter planes to blast British cities.

British RAF pilots were outnumbered and outgunned, but they had a secret technology called Chain Home. Chain Home was a line of radar stations. It used radio waves to spot incoming aircraft. This early warning system gave RAF commanders 20 minutes warning about where *Luftwaffe* squadrons were headed. They could then send fighters where they were most needed. Chain Home helped block German plans to invade.

FLYING BOMBS AND FIGHTER JETS

After early victories, German forces were in full retreat by June 1944. Still, German engineers were firing up new weapons. One was the V-1 flying bomb. Powered by a newfangled jet engine, it could strike targets more than 150 miles (240 km) away. Then came the V-2 rocket, the world's first long-range guided missile. In 1944 the *Luftwaffe* also flew the first fighter jet into battle, the Messerschmitt 262. But these advances came too late to prevent Nazi Germany's defeat.

 **FIGHTING FACT** RADAR stands for "Radio Detection and Ranging."

THE NAZI ROCKET SCIENTIST

Wernher von Braun was a member of the Nazi Party. He was also a genius of rocket science who oversaw the building of Germany's V-2 missile. He surrendered to the Americans immediately after the war. He and other German engineers were then transferred to the U.S. He later became the chief designer of the *Saturn V* rocket that launched U.S. astronauts to the moon.

A V-1 bomb lands in a street off Drury lane in london.

BOOTS FROM THE SKY

Most land battles depended on "grunts"—**infantry** troops. Both sides experimented with strapping troops in parachutes and dropping them behind enemy lines. Often, though, these paratroopers landed far from their intended targets.

Still, paratroopers played an important role during Operation Overlord. This was the Allied invasion in June 1944 to retake France. Dropped the night of June 6, paratroopers caused chaos behind German lines. They destroyed bridges and blocked roads to slow German **reinforcements**. This helped more than 150,000 Allied infantry come ashore near Normandy, France.

✓ Normandy Invasion

infantry—a group of soldiers trained to fight and travel on foot

reinforcements—extra troops sent to strengthen a fighting force

LAND MINES AND "BOUNCING BETTIES"

World War II saw widespread use of land mines. These were buried bombs that exploded when soldiers stepped on them. Anti-tank mines were also used to wreck advancing armor. The German S-mine proved very effective at slowing Allied infantry advances. Nicknamed "Bouncing Betty," it sprang into the air before exploding. One U.S. officer described the S-mine as "probably the most feared device encountered by Allied troops in the war."

FIGHTING FACT

New technology introduced at Normandy on D-Day included a "swimming" tank, a flame-throwing tank called "the crocodile," and collapsible motorbikes.

THE RACE FOR THE ATOMIC BOMB

In the 1930s scientists realized **atomic** weapons could release tremendous power. Leaders on all sides soon recognized that whatever country possessed such weapons would win the war.

The Manhattan Project was the most top-secret Allied program of World War II. An international team of more than 130,000 people worked on it, mainly in the U.S. Most did not even know the project's purpose—to build the first atomic bomb. American leaders feared Germany or the Soviet Union might beat them to it. The first atomic bomb was tested in New Mexico on July 16, 1945. The shock wave shattered windows in Silver City—120 miles (193 km) away.

An aerial view of Tachikawa, Japan, shows ruin left by bombing raids.

LITTLE BOY AND FAT MAN

In early May 1945 the Germans surrendered, ending the war in Europe. The Japanese were in retreat but still continued to fight. On August 6, a single U.S. bomber flew over Hiroshima, Japan. Minutes later there was a blinding flash and unbelievable explosion. The atomic bomb nicknamed "Little Boy" flattened the city in an instant. An estimated 80,000 people or more were killed. Three days later, another U.S. plane dropped the "Fat Man" atomic bomb on Nagasaki. It killed tens of thousands more. Japan surrendered a few days later.

post-war model → of an atomic bomb

FIGHTING FACT Spies for the Soviet Union stole important information from the Manhattan Project. The Soviets tested their own atomic bomb in 1949.

atomic—relating to or concerned with atoms, atomic bombs, or nuclear energy

THE DEADLIEST WAR

World War II was the deadliest, most destructive war in history—before or since. In earlier conflicts, military forces mainly targeted each other. The "total war" strategies of World War II broke all those rules.

Historians calculate anywhere from 50 to 85 million people died during World War II. They estimate civilians may have made up two-thirds of the dead. In the case of the Holocaust, innocent people were murdered just because of who they were. Bombing raids burned entire cities to the ground in Germany and Japan.

Secrets of all kinds were part of the fighting of World War II. Some secrets and deceptions killed while others saved lives. Soon after the end of World War II, though, everyone saw the truth about the next world war. If fought with atomic weapons, it could be the last war of all.

Country	Population that died (millions)
China	20,000,000
USSR	16,825,000
Germany	9,000,000
Ukraine	6,850,000
Poland	5,820,000
Japan	3,120,000
Berlarus	2,290,000
France	550,000
Italy	454,600
UK	450,900
US	420,000
Lithuania	375,000
Latvia	260,000
Canada	45,400

population that died (millions)

GLOSSARY

atomic (uh-TOM-ik)—relating to or concerned with atoms, atomic bombs, or nuclear energy

besiege (be-SEEJ)—to surround with armed forces

civilian (si-VIL-yuhn)—a person who is not in the military

commando (kuh-MAND-oh)—specially trained soldier used for secret missions

cryptologist (KYP-tol-uh-jist)—someone who studies codes

deception (di-SEP-shuhn)—something that makes people believe what is not true; a lie

decipher (di-SYE-fur)—to figure out something that is written in code or is hard to understand

deport (di-PORT)—to forcefully send someone out of the country

Holocaust (HAHL-uh-kost)—the killing of millions of Jews and other people by the Nazis during World War II

infantry (IN-fuhn-tree)—a group of soldiers trained to fight and travel on foot

neutral (NOO-truhl)—not supporting or agreeing with either side of a disagreement or competition

occupy (AHK-yuh-pye)—to take possession or control by military invasion

reinforcements (ree-in-FORSS-muhnts)—extra troops sent to strengthen a fighting force

ultimate (UHL-tuh-mit)—greatest, most important

CRITICAL THINKING USING THE COMMON CORE

1. Read the text on page 15. Why were the Navajo Code Talkers a valuable resource for the U.S. military? (Key Ideas and Details)

2. The Holocaust was a horrible event in human history. What happened during the Holocaust? (Craft and Structure)

READ MORE

Burgan, Michael. *World War II Spies: An Interactive History Adventure*. Mankato, Minn.: Capstone Press, 2013.

Chrisp, Peter. *The Story of the Second World War for Children*. London: Carlton Kids, 2016.

Throp, Claire. *Spies and Codebreakers. Heroes of World War II*. Mankato, Minn.: Capstone Press, 2015.

INTERNET SITES

FactHound offers a safe, fun way to find Internet sites related to this book. All of the sites on FactHound have been researched by our staff.

Here's all you do:

Visit *www.facthound.com*

FactHound will fetch
the best sites for you!

INDEX